FINISHING LINE PRESS

www.finishinglinepress.com

Mortal Beings

Kathleen —
Thanks for pausing
to consider life and mortality
Cynthia
5/23/19

poems by

Cynthia Trenshaw

Finishing Line Press
Georgetown, Kentucky

Mortal Beings

Naught is possessed, neither gold,
nor land nor love,
nor life, nor peace,
nor even sorrow nor death,
nor yet salvation.

Say of nothing: It is mine.
Say only: It is with me.
                    D. H. Lawrence

ACKNOWLEDGMENTS

I am grateful to the journals that first published the following poems:

Ellen and the Full Moon (*Peacock Journal*, January 2019)
Epilogue (Yellow Chair Press—*In the Words of Womyn International,* 2016
    Anthology)
Four Invisibilities (*The Main Street Rag*, Fall 2016)
Leaving My Mark (*A Quiet Courage*, January 2016)
Legerdemain (*Hospital Drive—UVA School of Medicine Journal*, February
    2017)
Off Bourbon Street (*Peacock Journal*, January 2019)
Piss (*Hospital Drive—UVA School of Medicine Journal*, February 2017)
Prism (*Redheaded Stepchild Magazine*, Winter 2018)
Recall Notice (*Snapdragon Journal*, September 2017)
Too Much to Lose (*Soundings Review*, Spring/Summer 2012)

Thanks to the many friends who listened, sighed, chuckled, and wept in all
the right places, and encouraged me often enough that I kept writing.

And forever gratitude to copyeditor Marian Blue who received my best-
I-could-make-them drafts and, with a few discerning comments and
suggestions, turned dross into richness.

Publisher: Leah Maines
Editor: Christen Kincaid
Cover Photo: Corrine Bayley
Author Photo: Dr. Chris Mann
Cover Design: Leah Huete

Printed in the USA on acid-free paper.
Order online: www.finishinglinepress.com
        also available on amazon.com

Author inquiries and mail orders:
Finishing Line Press
P. O. Box 1626
Georgetown, Kentucky 40324
U. S. A.

Table of Contents

LEGERDEMAIN

It's not the body
            afterward
    that fascinates me,
    though I'll wash the corpse with herbs and fragrant oils
    in flower-petaled water.
    I'll dress the cooling, stiffening limbs
    and wish the body's soul
    a gentle journey.

It's not the struggle
            during
    that compels me,
    though I'll have seen the body's poetry
    before the struggle ends:
    I'll wonder at the left foot calloused so,
    and hold the hand with jagged scar or
    missing thumb;
    I'll read the tales that limn the face
    and tiny crystal details
    sparkling in the fading eyes.
    I'll bring more morphine,
    moisten pasty lips and tongue,
    watch the belly rise and fail
    to pull air past the gurgling sounds,
    anticipate the inhale never followed
    by another.

It's not the awe of Death
            nearby
    that draws me,
    but that always it arrives unseen
    while I still wait its coming.
    And when I understand the moment's
    come, it's gone,
    the sacred glue already vaporized,
    life detached from flesh,
    abandoned cells deflating,
    blood settling to covert bruises,
    leaving frozen eyes
    and skin the hue of corn-silk
    or of wood ash.

It is that magic trick
               right before
my eyes that I can't grasp,
that brings me back again
(just one more time) to catch
Death's sleight of hand,
when *is* has changed to *was*
beneath the sheet.
And I'd not appreciate the irony
if, when I finally see the switch,
it happens in my body;
if at last I know the wizard's trick
but have no breath
with which to tell.

ONCE I BREATHED

Once I breathed the exhalation
         of a 30-ton gray whale,
         tiny molecules that reeked of krill
         and low-tide sulfur
         sucked into my astonished lungs.

Once I breathed in smoke and ash, residue
         of wildfires consuming
         half a million forest acres;
         of final filtered exhales
         from perished smokejumpers;
         of groans and dust of roofs collapsing;
         and the wails
         of fleeing residents.

Once I inhaled the pong
         of a homeless encampment
         constructed on a toxic waste heap.
         The stench stayed in my head for days
         but I went back
         to breathe it in again.

Once I breathed in some (perhaps more than my fair share)
         of the world's precious supply
         of the last breath of a friend
         who chose to die
         when the pain was unrelenting.

Once I wanted the metallic tang of shrieking train brakes
         to be the final
         molecules I ever breathed.

Mathematicians have estimated at 98.2%
the chances that at least one molecule in each of our inhales
         was first contained
         in *Et tu, Brute?*
         or *Forgive them, Father.*
         Knowing this, and near the end
         of my calculated allotment
         of seven hundred million breaths,
         I pay more attention now

to what I say: my legacy,
bequest of molecules
to those who may inhale from time to time
the fragrance of my life.

OFF BOURBON STREET

Gray stone walls hold a thousand months of sultry tales.
Dusty handmade bricks are held together by a dozen decades
of sweat and careful tuckpoint.
French Quarter's *signe distinctif* is black wrought iron,
metal forged and conjured
into curled black flowers and iron vines
by spells that make those growing things
immobile for your pleasure.

Behind a certain tall wrought gate,
deep in a back street often overlooked,
the splash-and-echo of a hidden fountain beckons.
Sound grows sharper with your curiosity,
street sounds dampened by the passageway
whose job it is to escort you
from one existence to this other.

Earlier you thought you knew
where you were headed,
but The Quarter has a different plan
tucked up her Creole sleeve.
She has plucked you here to toy with you
in a   cumin
                    chickory
                            remoulade
                                    beignet
            delta-flow
                    saxophone
                            lace-garter
                                    rum and fruit and mint
        swaying
                    mystic
                            candle-flicker
                                    ritual coitus,
deep inside that hidden fountained *jardin*.

Then without a single word of *bien merci* or *aréwar*,
and certainly no *désolé*,
she'll toss you out again—bemused, confused,
amnesic and forever changed—
onto the sunlit avenue
from which she lured you.

PRISM

A beveled edge of mirror snags
a sunray, throws it, breaks it
into crayon colors on my wall.

I want
to explore the colors.
I want
to learn their language.
I want
to be one of them.

As the family's closet mystic
my young mind was sure
the fractured light
was made of holy stuff
though I'd been taught to be
contemptuous of anything called "holy"
and anyone who used that word.

I want
to dive into the colors.
I want
to feel them stroke my naked skin.
I want
to swim in color, breathe it without drowning.

But how? Where is a mentor
who can whisper "holy" in my ear
before I plunge,
be waiting for me when I rise
dripping and elated?

Earth slowly spun,
the mystical straight rainbow
crept along my wall
and faded solemnly.
I was daunted
by forbidden holiness
so I, too, crept away,
ashamed of my emergent yearning
as if they'd caught me in a corner
touching myself down there.

SLIPPERY SLOPE

The hill would've been perfect
  if it hadn't been so steep.
    The snow would've been ideal
      if the surface hadn't become pebbly ice.
      It would've been a great brave run
        if that frozen upright twig hadn't snagged
        the crossbar of my sled.

          My bloodied face
           shredded palms
            and torn clothes
             would've been heroic
              if there'd been anyone there to notice.

I would've been home in time for dinner
if I weren't crying, scared, helpless
to retrieve my waylaid sled
and find our way
in the falling
dark.

ASKING

You didn't ask.
If you had, I would have lied.
And then, if you'd stood by me,
in time I would have cried,
confessed how scared I'd been,
and yet how thrilled,
how hard it was
to keep my teenage secret
of the older men
who flattered me
and nuzzled me
and

        But you never asked.

Years later, when I asked you
and you lied,
I stood by you.
In time you cried,
and said, "You don't know
how hard it's been,
keeping this secret
all these years."

I said I'd go with you
to Al-Anon,
we'd do an intervention.
Two days later you denied
our conversation
ever happened.

        At least I had asked.

CHICAGO'S RANDOLPH STREET STATION, 5:10PM, JULY 1958

Commuters mob the grottoed entrance
to the interurban terminal,
part a veil of heady fragrance
raised by two-buck rose bouquets
mounded on each concrete stair
descending steeply from the street.
Black-mineral redolence of printer's ink
alerts rushed patrons to the evening's Tribune;
each one slaps the vendor's palm with change,
he slaps the folded paper into practiced armpit,
neither relay racer breaks their rhythm.
Aroma of rotisserie chicken entices from a stall
beside the deeply-shadowed platform,
mixes with stale beggar-scent,
and sweat, cologne, and aftershave
of boarding ticket-holders,
and optimistic ozone odor
snapping from electric lines that power
orange train cars, carrying commuters
slowly sliding homeward on the silver rails
of the Chicago, South Bend, and South Shore Line.

EAU DE STREET

A signature scent formulated
beneath the squalid undersides of freeways,
discerned by cops and social workers, anyone
who's breathed among the homeless.

Organic odor, essence of unwashed,
of epidermal cells permeating clothing fibers,
mixed with city fumes and toxins,
fixed in place by sweat and other body fluids.

This aroma bears a mineral, metallic note
like menstrual blood but not so wholesome,
a tincture of life infused on the streets,
effused from pores of the destitute.

The fragrance clings inside my nose, lingers
long after my hot shower, outlasts
heavy-cycle laundering, seeps into my sleep:
haunting perfume of poverty and poisons.

FOUR INVISIBILITIES

In hospitals the camouflage
is gowns, sheets, slippers,
dispensed alike to every
patient; names, dates, allergies,
and ailments in tiny code
on narrow wristbands.

In county jails the ruse
is cleverer—jumpsuits so blatantly stigmatic
that law-abiding citizens close their eyes
against the glare of neon orange guilt,
rendering the prisoners
no longer in evidence.

In a crumbling neighborhood
drapes are closed behind
cracked and unwashed windows,
shutting away from public view
a cancer-ridden woman
who wants no interference
in her dying.

Downtown
the homeless ones
sip
from hidden bottles,
sleep
in plain brown wrappers.

SILENT DIALOGUE

She has one remaining tooth,
and shivering, skinny limbs.
Her thin butt leans against
a downtown granite wall.
One spent paper coffee cup is clutched
against her heart, another cup
is outstretched, begging
for a drop of coin.

ME: *I want to shelter you,*
to bathe and pamper you,
ask my dentist to make teeth for you.
I want to listen to your story
until your inner cup is full
of your own worth and goodness.
But I don't know what to say.
I don't know how to cross
the space between us.
And so, irresolute and impotent,
I look away, walk past.

SHE: *You hesitated.*
And for a moment
I thought you saw me.
I was wrong.
You saw only brokenness,
thought that to endure me
you must change me.
You could at least have
left some change,
as reparation
for the put-down.

PRAYER LINE

"We'll pray for you."
A promise made, and kept.

Diagnoses, surgeries,
accidents and births and deaths,
jobs lost, loves lost, bank accounts and futures lost.
Pray for me, pray for him,
pray for them, their family, and all their doctors, too.
Pray for healing, comfort, a way
out, God's forgiveness.

The weight of any single ask
is no greater than a sparrow flying in
to grasp the phone line strung along a country road.
Small body, tiny feet, feather-weighted
wings and fluffy down. Not much to bear.

But then another sparrow comes to perch,
another and another.
Requests flock daily to the prayer line
until my spirit sags
beneath the weight of pain and need and fear.
So many sparrows.

At day's end I send out
a prayer of my own:
"God, call, please call these prayer sparrows
to Your holy aviary.
Touch them. Feed them grain
and gnats.
Give them water for their thirst
and some to splash in. Give them
sacred rest, and send them off refreshed
with Your blessing for their service."

In the morning,
on the empty phone line,
the day's first sparrow comes to perch.

SITTING VIGIL

No more do-ing now,
sitting with a dying one.
   Only be-ing here.

Jeanette

She is quietly undoing
everything.
Letting go of
everything.
Allowing the contents of
her carefully packed luggage
to now be disarranged,
discarded.
She experiments inside herself
by wadding up a neatly folded memory.
By loosening the ties
that have secured her to a future.
By unfastening her expectation
that this journey would look
different than it does.

Can she manage this with skill enough
that undoing will not
shred her soul in pain?
Can she, without flinching,
tug at the adhesive
that has fused her self
together all these years?

John

He was a trucker
and a cook,
a heavyweight,
her husband.
An unlikely one
to keep the vigil
gently, to leave to her
what inner doing must be done.

Yet hour after hour he sits
comfortably at her side,
as if they were out for a drive,
passing the miles in their well-used camper,
passing the time in their well-worn silence;
as if together they were noticing the passing scene,
confirming with a glance
that the other notices as well,
touching sometimes, sharing everything
as if by telepathy.

This dying is an inadvertent journey,
at the end of which they'll part.
Perhaps forever.
Who really knows?
But now they are together
as long as her itinerary will allow.
If she needs something, he brings it.
He does not hover anxiously,
asking what her wants are
(something, anything to do
to make him feel a part of it).
He understands the asking would draw her back
from her hesitating steps
toward the border
for which he has, as yet,
no passport.

And she must go.
It is time.

So he waits,
keeping the vigil
and his silence,
and comes as close to
doing this right
as any person can.

EPILOGUE

He's home and coming up to bed.
So familiar his gait, the way
when he's especially tired or maybe
had a second glass of wine with friends,
his left shoulder brushes the wallpaper
with every other step.
And there's the squeak in the ninth step
just below the landing
where the last three stairs
turn up to the right and to our room.

I'm discomfited to have him find me
on his side of our bed, the side with the phone
and the alarm clock. I almost slide over to mine,
but he's already there, beside me, appraising me,
his elbow on my pillow,
his right hand propping up his head,
his face no longer gaunt with pain.
I offer a silent apology
for moving to his side so soon. He grins.
It's okay, I hear. *And*, he reassures me,
I'm okay too.
He reaches out his left hand
to stroke my jaw line in his signature
gesture of endearment.

I smile, lean into his hand,
though now I'm the only one
on either side
of our bed.

HATTIE'S LAST CROSSING

In the middle of its scheduled run
between two shores of the Salish Sea
the *MV Walla Walla* slowed then stopped
as Hattie's friends and family brought her to the stern.
She weighed about four pounds,
three quarts of volume
carried in a woven wicker box,
biodegradable.

Hattie's friends and family
joked about her bossiness and laughed
about her quirks, then said goodbye
and dropped her overboard.
The Mate, standing by attentively, cap removed respectfully,
gave a subtle signal to the wheelhouse high above.
The Captain loosed the basso-profundo of the vessel's horn
three times across the waters of the Salish Sea,
leaving one vibrating space between each sounding.

Riptide of tears
hit, as Hattie's friends and family reached
for someone to embrace
while engines roared to life again, sent a roiling wake
propelling Hattie further from the boat.
The mourners turned away, holding one another
or shoving hands in pockets, finding
nothing else to do with them.

From the wheelhouse, through binoculars,
the Captain kept official watch till Hattie sank.
His funereal duties now discharged,
he announced pro forma gratitude
for patience of the passengers, and piloted the living,
seven minutes late, to their intended terminal.

PISS

He is 95, still strong, and wearing
diapers. He reckons it a good day
when he stands before a toilet
with the seat up
and produces
any more than dribbles.

She is 93. Her brain has corroded,
erasing all but little details
of her childhood in North Dakota,
and the Norwegian national anthem.
She wakes up shivering in soaked
ammonia-scented sheets and wonders
how that happened.

The two sit on their sun-porch, nodding off.
Their gray-muzzled cocker spaniel looks
from one face to the other, whines, then
squats and pees between their chairs.

An hour from now the man will decree, again,
that tomorrow the dog will be put down.

The man cannot piss a stream,
cannot suicide,
nor euthanize his wife.
At least he can
kill
that damned
incontinent
dog.

YELLOW CAT

Without a breeze to ruffle them
the grassy weeds move, just there.
He is crouched, leonine
in his suburban jungle,
each slowmo muscle
of his trembling flanks focused
on a single goal.
       The mouse, her movements
slight and fussy,
sniffs the ground
but not the air
that carries musk
of danger.

Too late, or perfectly, depending
on which side one is rooting for,
a flash of yellow fur explodes
then rises—string of rodent tail,
two tiny paws, and blood
drooping/twitching/dripping
from the feline mouth.
       I cannot cringe away.
So exquisite the choreography,
the coupling of guile and innocence,
it would insult both cat and mouse,
and nature that designed them,
if I fled before the final
gulp.

TOO MUCH TO LOSE

On the dim side of her sunlit door
a metal stepstool scraped aside,
and she loosed the folded walker
wedged tight beneath the doorknob.

Deadbolt slid and doorknob turned
and darkness leaked toward me across her welcome mat.

In the space between the lower edge of door
and the doorsill that defines her world,
a severed lizard tail was trapped,
a five-inch piece with yellow stripes.

I did not speak about the tail, nor mention
my unease in knowing it was caught beneath her door.

Over tea, the widow said she could not leave
this house and all it holds of antiques, storage boxes,
years of work and memories. I thought, *And dust
and junk and smell of cats and age and fear.*

As I left I heard the edge of door, the deadbolt,
stepstool, walker all slide back in place.

Low on the siding of the yellow house, just above the weeds,
a tailless lizard clung, still but for her pulsing throat.
I thought, *She'll grow another tail,*
believing what I'd heard somewhere.

It's two days later now. I've come again,
await the widow's rite of unsecuring.
The door between her world and mine chafes open;
reluctantly I glance down at the doorsill.

The tailless lizard lies, vacant-eyed and desiccating,
beside the tail she could not leave behind.

SAFELY STORED

She never remembered the closet again.
Once it was filled, she closed the door,
turned, and wandered away.
Slowly the dust took over.

Once it was filled, she closed the door.
Because she'd left her memory inside,
the dust took over, slowly
shrouding everything in thick soft gray.

Because she'd left her memory inside,
it was unchanging there, her biography
cloaked in years of thick soft gray,
safe from aging's desecration.

It was unchanging there, her biography.
She turned, and wandered away,
safe from aging's desecration.
She never remembered the closet again.

INJURED RABBIT

From my window I watch him
hunched in unmowed grasses.
He sucks dewdrops, nibbles tender parts of stalks,
turns gradually, three-hundred-sixty degrees,
his damaged left leg dragging as he rotates,
his eyes and radar ears alert for swoosh or shadow
of harrier or hawk, until he tires,
grows motionless, and dozes.

My phone rings. It's my friend with damaged
heart and shadow growing in his lung.
His three-hundred-sixty degrees
used to have a longer radius but now
he nibbles from the nearby fridge
spoonfuls of cold mac and cheese.
Calls friends, sits, and dozes.

Half an hour later, I check back on the rabbit.
I can barely spot where he had been.

BEWARE

Just below the edge where dune grass
peers down sloping sand—just there,
in swaying grassy shadows—
a shallow concave cone is dug,
no bigger round than this year's plums.

Stay a while, and study quietly.
Appreciate the balance.
Not a grain of sand falls
to the apex of that perfect construct

'til an inattentive ant
trips over the round hole's edge.

The ant begins its frantic
futile climb up sliding sand grain boulders.
The six-legged ant lion, alerted,
raises head and shoulders
from the center of the cone.
Two gray pincered arms
snatch the struggling guest
backward
into the dining room.

It's over in a heartbeat.
A final sand grain settles into place
and motionless perfection is restored
to an empty shallow sand cone
just below the edge of dune grass.
Waiting.

SOLAR ECLIPSE, ENGLAND, 1999

With walking sticks and fervor we climb the tor,
toting babies, picnics, dogs, to see the show.
A thick haze hides the sun from Devon's moor,
holds the day in eerie gray-mist glow.
Slowly, birds go silent, heartbeats quicken,
pall descends, festive mood abates.
Is this the sun's eclipse? Can daylight thicken?
Daunted dogs whimper, heel, and wait.

Is this the death of light? Mutely I wail
and beg deliverance from lowering doom.
Vestigial reptile-brain groans. Forebrain fails,
impotent in night-dark day at noon.
In every superstitious cell I pray,
Make our sun and light return this day.

PERMISSION

Hands deep in soapy water
absently feeling for another fork or spoon.
Staring out the kitchen window
mind pleasantly blank
before the sunny afternoon turns
into family time and supper preparation.

Back door flies open.
Tommy bursts in, as always,
enthused, breathless, holding out a paper,
some classroom note, or a permission slip.

Mom, there's this thing I want to do,
a great opportunity.
He pauses to gauge the reaction.
I've got this chance to go somewhere,
where I can ask ANYthing and learn EVERYthing,
everything I've ever wanted to know!
Please Mom, please can I go?

Face wet,
warm tears burst rainbow bubbles in the sink.
Tommy dead three months,
yet here, permission slip in hand,
eager. Knowing what he's asking.

You know too.

There's one thing though, Mom.
He hesitates, makes eye contact.
If I go, I can't ever come back.
But can I go, Mom? Can I?

Edge of sink supporting belly,
breathing stopped,
hands still in soapy water.
Impossible to speak around a choke.
You know the answer.

And so you nod.
And he is truly gone.

SUSAN'S DEATH WITH DIGNITY

My blouse was black, for grieving,
embroidered wildly, for celebration.
The day was that way too—
rain, then sun, and rain again,
with swirling mist
that seemed to promise rainbows.

Seven sat in circle by her wood stove:
Susan, too young and cancer-filled,
sitting in a rocker; her twenty-something son,
four friends, a volunteer who had experience,
and Ziggy, Susan's wheezy ancient dog.

Goodbyes said and blessings given,
it was time. We placed our chairs
around her bed. In case the dying
took a while, she made one final
bathroom stop, then sat on her bed's edge.

Curious even now, Susan chose to know
the taste of these compounded drugs.
She took the bitter cup
without a masking flavor,
drank it in three swallows
without a hesitation. Winced.

Her son, more grounded and transparent
than wise men thrice his age,
made her pillow comfortable, expressed his love,
held her hand, stroked the dog,
and wept his tender, quiet tears.

After twenty silent minutes
Susan's sacred ember flickered and went out.
Some said they saw
the moment that her spirit left.
I only saw her shallow breathing cease.

What else is one to do then,
except to leave forget-me-nots
on her stilled chest, make the necessary calls,
agree to let her bright body
be rolled away on a gray gurney.

Outside, the day opted for sunny.
I didn't notice any rainbows,
but I heard a spotted towhee sing.

ELLEN AND THE FULL MOON

The full moon always sets at dawn.
To grasp just how that happens, I need
an orange and a tennis ball,
a flashlight and an extra hand,
and lots of time to work it out.

Last week Ellen died, gazing at the full moon's setting.

In her waning, she waxed fully vital.
To grasp how that is possible, I'd need
a candle and a scrying ball,
perhaps a theologian and an oracle,
and lots of time to parse their explanations.

With her life nearing its horizon Ellen radiated
reverence for silence, awe, and endings.
She welcomed guests, and welcomed death as one of them
until at last, shining in her fullness,
she set with her beloved moon, at dawn.

RECALL NOTICE

A doctor shows me
lab reports,
spells out words I've never heard
and numbers meaningless to me.
She illustrates with diagrams
how somewhere in my inner coils
something's gone awry.

Do charted numbers
and manufactured words
mean anything at all?
If not, then why do I remember
only vaguely
who I was before them,
and whose is this obscure to-do list?

I had plans for autumn.
I'd smiled, imagining myself
determinedly
inching toward my goals,
leaving a hyphenated snail trail
glistening behind me
through the months of summer.

Now my plans for summer are
to curl inward,
to hang out with spirally friends
sheltering from sunlight,
clinging under damp dark flower pots
and pondering questions way too big
for gastropodous brains—
brains that don't remember much
beyond the needs of now
and how to make a shiny hyphen
on a moonlit garden path.

WABI SABI WARNING

You cannot do this right.
There is no "right" to be done.
I can't well articulate what's needed
and you have no way of guessing
and even if you guess right it will be wrong.
Because you cannot make me well again.

There's no such thing as perfect caring,
never ideal service. Never will they find
brightly-colored-anatomy-book groupings
of everything inside this bag of skin.

It's a messy job, trying to care for a friend.
It's a *wabi sabi* time
full of flaws and degradation,
transience and frustrating uncertainty.

If that's acceptable to you,
please stay with me, intrigued
by the unpredictability,
laughing with me in the dark humor.
Finding with me unlikely beauty,
and light squeezing through the chinks.
Awed with me by the blinks
of unexpected insight
we find in both of us.

But if you can't abide imperfection,
if you can't see the loveliness
in worn places, fissures, faded
fabric patched and darned
and sometimes damned,
then it's best you bow out now
because that's the material
that needs tending to,
and I'm the *wabi sabi* one you'll tend
even though I won't know what
I want nor how I want it,
and neither one of us can ever
do it right.

AIL

mortly afeart,
     frait some
          how I have
          off fended body gods
          come con damned
              by others—
              those ajudge
              and those who would afriend me
                  anyway

body in dis ease even tho
I ply with rules
     for well
     for heal

I magine pushed
     a sighed
     bandoned
          (a selfful feeling prophet)

so frayed
     so feart
     and so alonely

LEAVING MY MARK

As I recognize my shrinking span of days,
I'm not dismayed, much.
I'm content with who I am, mostly,
and what I've done, mostly.
My name will not be mentioned in syllabi
of any academic courses,
nor known beyond the memories
of two next generations,
and that's okay, I guess.

Sometimes, though, I have an urge
to rub my jowls against the doorjambs
and table legs of hence,
depositing me-scented markers
for passersby to sense
and wonder: *who <u>was</u> that?*

A DROP OF HOLY SILENCE

Like a housewife coaxing flies out of her kitchen
Sister Lucy gently shooed the noisy day away,
urged this weary traveler in and shut the door.

I was welcomed, fed,
then had my fill of sleep. When daylight came
I woke enveloped in a mystic element
like living dew or sacramental water:
a drop of deep and holy silence.
Effortlessly I sank into it.
No need to dive, nor struggle to discern
mysterious instructions from Divinity,
nor work at keeping thoughts
above a waterline.

Not floating,
not drowning, no effort to breathe
in that sphere of holy welcome
large enough to embrace me
small enough to be held in the palm of a nun's hand
solid enough to be carried in her pocket
as she went about her day
praying for me as she promised.

RAVEN'S GIFT

In the southeast corner of New Mexico
two nights' hard December freeze
left the critters of the Living Desert
Zoo free of visitors, except for me.
I stood before the cage marked "Raven."

A disarray of corvid toys
speckled the floor of his enclosure:
a ping pong ball, marbles, buttons, a box
with straw for stashing treasures in,
later to be dug out for his pleasure.

I spoke to Raven, expressing my regard,
my admiration of his clever kind.
He cocked his sleek head rightward, flew
from his perch and strutted toward me
with his cocky Raven gait.

He sized me up, considering,
then turned around, sorted through
his things, came back carrying
a shiny bauble in his beak,
dropped it just inside the fencing.

A gift for me! Thrilled, I reached
two fingers through the chicken-wire.
His beak drew blood
before I even touched the glass-clear offering.
Wound in mouth, sucking pain, I felt betrayed.

Raven cocked his sleek head leftward,
considering, as only Ravens can.
Picking up the shiny bead, he poked his beak
through wire fence and dropped the prize
on my side of our boundary line.

Warily, I reached again, retrieved
the piece—of ice!—chipped from water bowl,
now given for the healing of my Raven wound.
We stared intently, he and I, each as certain as
the other that I had just received

ravenitiation into his clan.

GRANDSON

We've not met in three years. He was ten then.
I've not changed much. He has.
He's six feet tall, not yet through puberty,
I'm stooped, white-haired, and long past menopause.
We have a week to spend together,
his first so far from home.
What kind of person
lives behind those lovely dark-fringed eyes?
What kind of person
studies him and wonders?
Will we judge each other? By whose standards?

Last night I named the diagnosis, told my grandson
of chronic subtle atrophies
that make my muscles older than my years.
He heard in silence, had no questions for me,
perhaps surprised he's old enough
to be confided in like that.

Morning dawns, Northwest gray and wet again,
rainforest and Pacific Coast ahead.
We hear the boom and sough of surf before we see it,
smell salty kelp and fainter scent
of granite being pulverized to sand.
A low dune lies between us and Rialto Beach.
Joseph picks his way through hulking driftwood, takes the lead,
silently assessing what I can and cannot do.
And then an impasse: huge gray storm-tossed trees
piled haphazardly across our path with no way past them.
He hesitates, surveys options, decides.

He plants his feet securely on two trunks,
extends his hand to mine. Our eyes connect before our hands do.
I find no judgment on his face, he finds no shame on mine.
Nothing now but touch of palm to palm,
an open portal, uterus of genealogy:
in him my lineage extends to who he'll be;
the heritage in his becoming salutes the woman who emerged
from all who came before.

Strong and proud, he helps me cross the barrier.
The moment closes: a womb finished with its work.
Waves crash before us, foam and spume surround us
in amniotic blessing.

Widowed at the age of 51, after 32 years of marriage, **Cynthia Trenshaw** soon recognized an opportunity to reinvent herself, and she grabbed that opportunity with gusto. In the next twenty years she completed her long-neglected bachelor's degree, and went on to earn a masters degree in theology. She became a nationally-certified hospital chaplain, a nationally-certified massage therapist, a state-certified professional guardian, and a nursing assistant-registered.

Cynthia's workplaces were one city's infamous slums and another city's hospital corridors and emergency room cubicles. She served people of all ages, from young children in a mental hospital to elders in a 210-bed nursing home. She encountered the "mortal beings" of her poems as a massage therapist among the street people of San Francisco, as a guardian ad litem in superior courtrooms, as a bedside caregiver for a residential hospice, and as a deep appreciator of the natural beauty that surrounds her in her Washington home.

In all of these experiences, Cynthia has paid attention, and brought her keen eye to the crafting of her poems about mortality. Nor does she shy from acknowledging herself as mortal; she draws richly from her own biography. Each experience featured in this collection of poems brings a combination of compassion and celebration, and no little amount of awe, to the acknowledgement that every beginning has an end, and every living thing is a mortal being.

Noticing is the first task of any poet, and the rest of the work is inviting the reader to see through the poet's eyes. It takes courage to notice mortality. Be courageous, and enter this book; enter the world of Cynthia Trenshaw.